THERE'S A FLY IN MY SOUP!

SANDY RANSFORD has been hooked on humour ever since her first job in publishing – editing the jokes for a well-known magazine – and she has now written more joke books than she can count. Born in South Yorkshire (which may account for it), she now lives in rural mid-Wales surrounded by sheep, with her husband, a horse, a cat, two pygmy goats and two miniature ponies – all of which keep her laughing.

JANE ECCLES is a prolific and talented illustrator. She lives in London with her husband, her son Theo and a great many plants. She has just adopted a rescue cat.

Also published by Macmillan

ALIEN JOKES
by Sandy Ransford

FOOTBALL JOKES
by Sandy Ransford

THE KNOCK KNOCK JOKE BOOK
by Sandy Ransford

2001: A JOKE ODYSSEY
THE MILLENNIUM JOKE BOOK
by Sandy Ransford

SPOOKY JOKES
by Sandy Ransford

CHRISTMAS JOKES
by Sandy Ransford

SCHOOL JOKES
by Sandy Ransford

THERE'S A FLY IN MY SOUP!

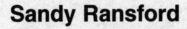

Sandy Ransford

Illustrated by **Jane Eccles**

MACMILLAN CHILDREN'S BOOKS

First published 2001 by Macmillan Children's Books

This edition produced for
The Book People Ltd,
Hall Wood Avenue, Haydock,
St Helens WA11 9UL

ISBN 0 330 48350 1

3 5 7 9 8 6 4 2

A CIP catalogue record for this book is available from the British Library.

Printed by Mackays of Chatham plc, Chatham, Kent.

Contents

Rise and Shine

What do cats eat for breakfast?
Mice krispies.

What do French children eat for breakfast?
Huit heures bix.

What's the best day to eat bacon and eggs?
Fry-day.

Two flies were on a cereal packet. 'Why are
we running so fast?' asked the first.
**'Because,' replied his friend, 'it says
"tear along the dotted line".'**

What did one cornflake say to the other?
'Cereal pleasure to meet you.'

BILL: There's a lot of juice in this grapefruit.
GILL: Yes, there's more than meets the eye.

What would
happen if pigs
could fly?
**Bacon would
go up.**

ANNE: Have you
heard the joke about
the eggs?
DAN: No.
ANNE: Two bad.

What goes up brown or white and comes
down yellow and white?
An egg.

BEN: Is it correct to say, 'The yolk of an
egg is white', or 'The yolk of an egg are
white'?
KEN: 'The yolk of an egg is white'.
BEN: Rubbish! The yolk of an egg is yellow!

Why do sausages have no manners?
They spit in the frying pan.

MAN IN CAFÉ: This egg's bad.
WAITRESS: Don't blame me. I only laid the table.

What do you call a naughty egg?
A practical yolker.

What did the toaster say to the loaf?
'Pop up and see me sometime.'

Why are mushrooms like umbrellas?
They spring up when it's wet.

ACTOR: I was once in a play called *Breakfast in Bed*.
ACTRESS: Did you have a big role?
ACTOR: No, just a slice of toast and marmalade.

A man stopped at a transport café for breakfast. 'What can I get you?' asked the waitress.

'I'll have some leathery bacon, half-cooked

sausages, a greasy egg and some dried-up old mushrooms,' he replied.

'We couldn't possibly serve you food like that!' exclaimed the waitress.

'Why not?' asked the man. 'You did yesterday.'

Knock, knock.
Who's there?
Egbert.
Egbert who?
Egbert no bacon.

What happens when you eat yeast and boot polish?
You rise and shine.

How does a coffee pot feel when it's full?
Perky.

'Yuck! This coffee tastes like mud!'
'Well, it was ground this morning.'

FIRST MAN IN CAFÉ: Is this coffee or tea? It tastes like dishwater.
SECOND MAN IN CAFÉ: Then it's tea. The coffee tastes like paraffin.

11

SIGN IN A CAFÉ: Don't complain about the tea. You may be old and weak yourself one day.

LADY IN CAFÉ: May I have coffee without milk, please?
WAITRESS: We're out of milk. Will you have it without cream?

JENNY: Mum, this egg tastes funny.
MOTHER: Then why aren't you laughing?

Why is honey scarce in Birmingham?
Because there's only one B in Birmingham.

Why was the strawberry worried?
Because his pals were in a jam.

CLARA: Did you hear the joke about the bread?
SARA: No.
CLARA: Oh, crumbs.

What did Dracula have at 11 o'clock each morning?
A coffin break.

JOHNNY: Mum, I can't eat this food.
MOTHER: Why not?
JOHNNY: You haven't given me a knife and fork.

TRAMP IN STREET: Got 50p for a cup of tea, guv?

MAN PASSING BY: No.

TRAMP: Blimey! You'd better take my mouth-organ, you're worse off than I am!

Have you read *Cooking Breakfast* by Egon Bacon?

Or *Continental Breakfast* by Roland Butter?

Out to Lunch

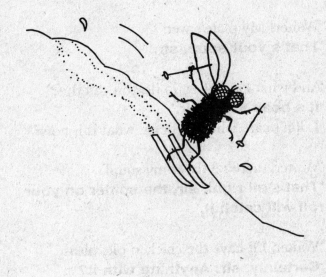

'Waiter!
There's a fly
in my soup!'
**'They don't
seem to care
what they eat
nowadays, do
they?'**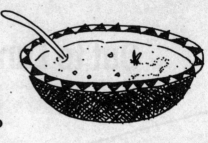

'Waiter! My plate's wet!'
'That's your soup, sir.'

'And what kind of soup do you call this?'
'It's bean soup, sir.'
'I don't care what it's been, what is it now?'

'Waiter, there's a fly in my soup!'
**'That's all right, sir, the spider on your
roll will catch it.'**

'Waiter, I'll have the chicken pie, please.'
'Certainly, sir. Anything with it?'
'Well, if it's anything like last week's, a
hammer and chisel would come in handy.'

'Waiter, I'd like the soup and the fish, please.'
**'If I were you, sir, I'd have the fish first,
it's on the turn.'**

'Waiter, what's the matter with this fish?'
'Long time, no sea, sir.'

'Waiter, why's my food all mushy?'
**'You did ask me to step on it,
sir.'**

'Waiter, there isn't
any chicken in this
chicken pie.'
**'There aren't any
shepherds
in the shepherd's
pie, either, sir.'**

'Waiter, will my omelette be
long?'
'No, sir, round.'

'And how did you find your steak, sir?'
**'Oh, I just moved a chip and there it
was.'**

'I'll have the roast lamb, please.'
**'And what will you have afterwards,
sir?'**
'Well, if it's anything like yesterday's,
indigestion, I expect.'

'Waiter, I'd like an elephant sandwich, please.'
'I'm sorry, sir, we can't do elephant sandwiches.'
'Why not?'
'We've run out of bread.'

'Waiter, why is there a button in my salad?'
'It's from the jacket potato, sir.'

'Waiter, have you frogs' legs?'
'No, sir, it's just the way I walk.'

'I'll have the plaice, please, and a glass of white wine.'
'Fillet, sir?'
'Of course, to the top of the glass.'

'Help! What have I just
eaten?'
'Cottage pie, sir.'
'Well, call a doctor, I think
I've just swallowed a
window pane.'

'Waiter, my lemonade's all
cloudy.'
**'No, sir, it's just the
glass that's dirty.'**

'Waiter, your thumb's
in my soup.'
'That's all right, sir, it's not hot.'

'I think I'll have the pork chop – no, make
that the cod steak.'
'I'm a waiter, sir, not a magician.'

'Waiter, have you smoked eels?'
'No, sir, just cigars.'

'Waiter, the crust on that steak pie was very
tough.'
**'That wasn't the crust, sir, you've eaten
the paper plate.'**

'Waiter, this curry is terrible.'
'But, sir, the chef here has been making curry since before you were born.'
'Maybe, but why did he have to save it for me?'

'What's that fly doing on my ice cream?'
'Learning to ski, sir.'

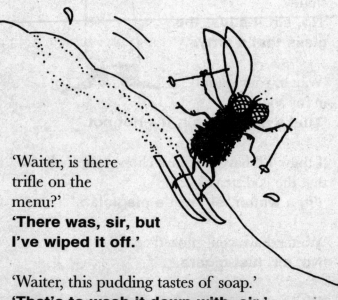

'Waiter, is there trifle on the menu?'
'There was, sir, but I've wiped it off.'

'Waiter, this pudding tastes of soap.'
'That's to wash it down with, sir.'

'Waiter, you've brought me the wrong order.'
'Well, sir, you did ask for something different.'

'Waiter, I can't eat this food. Get me the manager.'
'He won't eat it either, sir.'

'Waiter, there's only one piece of meat in my stew.'
'I'll cut it in two for you, sir.'

'Waiter, how long will my sausages be?'
'About 10 centimetres, sir.'

'Waiter, there's a film on my soup.'
'Have you seen it before, sir?'

'Waiter, there's a frog in my soup.'
'Yes, sir, the fly's on holiday.'

'Waiter, there's a twig in my soup.'
'Yes, sir, we have branches everywhere.'

'We have almost everything on the menu, sir.'
'So I see. Could you bring me a clean one, please?'

'Waiter, there's a beetle in my soup.'
'It must have committed insecticide, sir.'

'Waiter, there's a dead wasp in my soup.'
'What do you expect for 50p, sir, a live one?'

'Waiter, I've been waiting an hour for my turtle soup.'
'Sorry, sir, but you know how slow turtles are.'

'Waiter, there's an eggshell in my soup.'
'Well, it is birds'-nest soup, sir.'

'Waiter, this food's terrible. Bring me the manager.'
'He won't taste any better, sir.'

'Waiter, I think I'd like a little game.'
'Shall I bring a pack of cards, sir?'

'Waiter, why have you got your thumb on my steak?'
'To stop it falling on the floor again, sir.'

School Dinners

NICK: It's Enthusiasm Stew for
dinner again.
**DICK: What's
Enthusiasm Stew?**
NICK: It's when the
cook puts everything
she's got into it.

What's the difference between school tapioca
pudding and frogspawn?
Not a lot.

What's yellow, lumpy and stupid?
Thick school custard.

What's the best place to have the school
sickroom?
Next to the canteen!

What's school rhubarb?
Celery with high blood pressure.

TEACHER: Now eat up your cabbage, Melissa, it'll put colour in your cheeks.

MELISSA: But I don't want green cheeks!

ANDY: I thought there was a choice for dinner today.

DINNER LADY: There is.

ANDY: No there isn't, there's just fish.

DINNER LADY: You can choose to eat it or leave it.

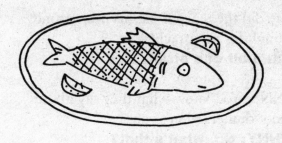

Why are school cooks cruel?

Because they batter fish and beat eggs.

TEACHER TO DINNER LADY: I'll have a chop, please, and make it lean.

DINNER LADY: Certainly, Mr Rumbletum, to the right or to the left?

TEACHER: Eat up your meat, Johnny, it's full of iron.
JOHNNY: No wonder it's so tough.

How do you save school dumplings from drowning?
Put them in gravy boats.

NELLIE: Our school must have very clean kitchens.
KELLY: Why do you say that?
NELLIE: All the food tastes of soap.

How did the teacher eat his minestrone through his moustache?
With a bit of a strain.

JENNY: You know what they say about school dinners, don't you?
PENNY: No, what's that?
JENNY: What goes down, must come up!

A teacher was trying to teach her class good table manners. 'Now, children, remember,' she said, 'a polite boy or girl never crumbles their bread or rolls in their soup.'

How does the school salad say grace?
'Lettuce pray.'

SUSIE: Are slugs nice to eat, Miss?
**TEACHER: Don't be disgusting, Susie.
Eat up your dinner and I'll speak to you
later.**
**TEACHER, LATER: Now, Susie, what
was it you wanted?**
SUSIE: I wondered if slugs were nice to eat,
Miss, but it's too late now. There was one on
your lettuce but it's gone.

Why did the school blancmange wobble?
Because it saw the milk shake.

TEACHER: Eat up your carrots, Herbert, they're good for your eyes.
HERBERT: How do you know?
TEACHER: Well, have you ever seen a rabbit wearing glasses?

What should children do when there are rock cakes for lunch?
Take their pick.

What should would-be athletes eat for school dinner?
Runner beans.

MANDY: If you eat any more you'll burst.
ANDY: Then you'd better watch out, I'm going to have some pudding.

Why did the daft boy have a sausage behind his ear?
Because he'd eaten his pencil at lunchtime.

Did you hear about the school that makes its own yoghurt? They just keep the milk for a few days and then get the ugliest teacher to sit and stare at it.

TEACHER, IN
DINING ROOM:
Order, children, order!
**PUPILS: Ice creams
all round, please!**

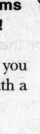

What do you get if you
cross school jelly with a
sheepdog?
Collie-wobbles.

There was a young man of St Just
Who ate apple pie 'til he bust.
It wasn't the fru-it
That caused him to do it,
What finished him off was the crust.

What did the children in the sculpture class
eat?
Marble cake.

What should a schoolboy eat if he wants to
be big and strong?
Mussels and brawn.

How do Welsh children eat cheese?
Caerphilly.

What musical instrument goes with cheese?
Pickle-o.

BEN: Why aren't you eating your
hamburger?
**KEN: I'm waiting for the mustard to
cool.**

TEACHER: Don't eat your food so quickly,
Bertie.
**BERTIE: But I might lose my appetite
unless I do.**

PADDY: Fish is supposed to be very good for
the brain.
MADDIE: I know. I eat lots of it.
PADDY: So much for that theory then.

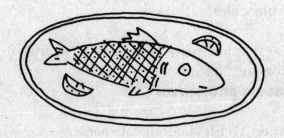

TEACHER: Eat up your salad, Samantha, it's good for growing children.
SAMANTHA: But who wants to grow children?

FUSSY CHILD: I don't like cheese with holes in.
TEACHER: Well leave the holes at the side of your plate and eat the rest.

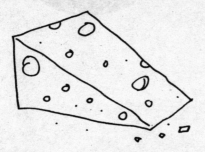

Two children were discussing school food. 'Ours is terrible,' said the first.

'You should taste ours,' said the second. 'We're the only school whose dustbins have indigestion.'

KAREN: Our school meals usually consist of UFOs.
SHARON: What do you mean?
KAREN: Unidentified Frying Objects.

Foul Food

What's worse than finding a slug in your salad sandwich?
Finding half a slug!

What's a vampire's favourite fruit?
A blood orange.

SIGN IN A DELICATESSEN:
Our tongue sandwiches speak for themselves.

What did the mouse say when it broke its front teeth?
'Hard cheese.'

How can you help a starving cannibal?
Give him a hand.

What's a cannibal's favourite wine?
One with lots of body.

CANNIBAL HUSBAND: I've brought a friend home for lunch.
CANNIBAL WIFE: You might have warned me. I've spent all morning making a stew.

What *is* the definition of a cannibal?
**Someone who goes into a restaurant
and orders the chef.**

'Mummy, mummy, I don't like Grandad.'
'Well just eat your chips then, dear.'

Little Miss Muffet
Sat on a tuffet
Eating her Irish stew,
Along came a spider
And sat down beside her,
And so she ate him up, too.

Knock, knock.
Who's there?
Aida.
Aida who?
Aida pound of green apples and now I've got
tummy ache.

NOSY NEIGHBOUR, LOOKING OVER FENCE: What are you going to do with all that manure?

GARDENING NEIGHBOUR: Put it on my strawberries.

NOSY NEIGHBOUR: Really? I always have cream on mine!

GRANDAD: Yesterday's lunch was terrible. I hope you're going to give me something today that I can get my teeth into.

GRANDMA: I certainly am. Here's a glass of water.

Where does a chicken go when it dies?
To oven.

MUM: I've made the chicken soup.
MIN: Thank goodness we don't have to eat it.

JOHN: Does an apple a day really keep the doctor away?
DON: It does if your aim is good enough.

TIM: If an apple a day keeps the doctor away, what does an onion a day do?
JIM: I don't know, what does it do?
TIM: Keeps everyone away!

Why did the lobster blush?
Because it saw the salad dressing.

CHARLENE: Would you like some nougat?
MARLENE: It's pronounced 'noogar'. The T is silent.
CHARLENE: Not the way you drink yours it isn't!

What's a cannibal's favourite supper?
Fish and chaps.

What did the cannibal say to the famous explorer?
'Dr Livingstone, I consume?'

A cannibal was about to cook his latest victim for his chief's supper, but before he did so he decided to ask him what his job was.

'I'm assistant editor on the *Daily News*,' replied the victim.

'Is that so?' said the cannibal. 'Well, you'll soon be editor-in-chief.'

What happened to the cannibals who ate the comedian?
They had a feast of fun.

What do cannibals do at a wedding?
Toast the bride and groom.

What are the best things to put in a pie?
Your teeth.

What do monsters eat with bread and cheese?
Pickled organs.

GIRL IN CINEMA: Oooh, this film gives me a cold, slithery feeling all down the back of my neck!
HER BOYFRIEND: So that's where my ice cream went!

'Mummy, Mummy, what's a vampire?'
'Shut up and drink your soup before it clots.'

What happens if you play badminton with a bad egg?
First it goes ping, then it goes pong.

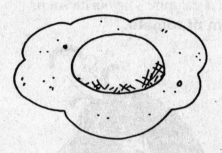

MR FAT-TUM: This meat's tough. What is it?
MRS FAT-TUM: Wood pigeon.
MR FAT-TUM: In that case I'll get my saw.

MR JELLYBELLY: There's a hair in this honey cake.
MRS JELLYBELLY: It must have come off the comb.

What do you get if you eat uranium?
Atomic ache.

What do ghosts like on their roast beef?
Grave-y.

Did you hear about the dog that ate only garlic and onions?
Its bark was worse than its bite.

What's a vampire's favourite soup?
Scream of tomato.

ARCHIMEDES: Eureka!
ARCHIMEDES' NEIGHBOUR: What of?
ARCHIMEDES: Garlic!

TEACHER: Cuthbert! Go and wash your face. I can see what you had for breakfast round your mouth.
CUTHBERT: What did I have?
TEACHER: It looks like fried eggs.
CUTHBERT: Wrong! That was yesterday.

MR ROUNDTUM: This casserole's half cold.
MRS ROUNDTUM: Well, eat the half that's hot.

ANDY: What's the difference between a hamburger and a dead mouse?
MANDY: I don't know.
ANDY: In that case I'll eat the hamburger and you can have the mouse.

What's a vampire's favourite breakfast cereal?
Ready-neck.

What's a vampire's favourite dessert?
Leeches and scream.

Off Your Trolley

A lady walked into a greengrocer's in a very smart district of London and was appalled to be charged £4 for a bag of apples. She handed the assistant a £5 note and began to walk towards the door. The assistant called after her, 'Madam, you've forgotten your change.'

The shopper turned round. 'You'd better keep it,' she replied, 'I trod on a grape on my way in.'

SHOPPER: Do you have pigs' trotters?
BUTCHER: No, madam, I walk this way because my shoes are too tight.

SHOPPER: How much are your chickens?
BUTCHER: £2 a pound.
SHOPPER: Did you raise them yourself?
BUTCHER: Oh, yes, they were £1.50 a pound this morning.

Late one Christmas Eve Mrs Biggles went to her butcher to buy a turkey. The butcher only had one turkey left. He showed it to Mrs Biggles who looked at it and said, 'I really wanted something larger. Have you got one?'

So the butcher took the turkey to the back of the shop, plumped it up a bit and brought it back. 'Just this one, madam,' he said.

'Hmm,' said Mrs Biggles, 'I'm not sure that's big enough either. I tell you what, I'll take both of them.'

BUTCHER: We've got some good pork in today.

HIS ASSISTANT: Don't talk chop.

An angry woman went into a butcher's shop and said, 'That meat you sold me last week was dreadful!'

'What was wrong with it?' asked the butcher. 'Was it tough?'

'I'll say!' replied the woman. 'I couldn't even get my fork into the gravy!'

MOTHER: Did you wash that fish you bought today before you cooked it?

FATHER: What's the point of washing something that's spent its life in water?

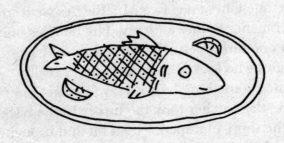

Why are bakers silly?

Because they sell what they knead.

Why do bakers work hard?
To earn an honest crust.

A man walked into a fishmonger's and asked the assistant to throw him six large trout.

'Why do you want me to throw them to you?' asked the assistant.

'I went fishing today and caught nothing,' replied the man. 'And I don't like telling lies. So this way I can truthfully say I caught six fine trout.'

Two shoppers were looking at the fishmonger's window. 'That salmon looks nice,' said the first.

'That's not salmon,' retorted the second. 'That's cod blushing at the price they're asking for it.'

SUSIE: Mum, can I have some money for the man who's crying outside?
MUM: Yes, but what's he crying about?
SUSIE: He's crying, 'Ice cream, ice cream!'

A girl went to the baker's to buy a loaf of bread. 'Is that all?' enquired the baker.
  'No,' replied the girl shyly. 'Mum says will you slice it for us, please, er – with a jammy knife.'

What's white or brown outside, green inside, and hops?
A frog sandwich.

ALICE: I love the bread from Mr Crumbs the baker's, don't you? It's always so lovely and warm.
ALAN: That's because Mr Crumbs' cat, Tiddles, sits on it all day.

What do elves order at the baker's?
Fairy cakes.

MÆVE: Try a slice of this cake I bought this morning.

DAVE: Ugh! It tastes horrible!

MÆVE: You have no taste. The wrapper says quite plainly that it's delicious.

NAUGHTY NORA: Have you any broken biscuits?

SHOPKEEPER: Yes.

NAUGHTY NORA: Well, you should be more careful, then.

Three friends went into a sweetshop. The first asked for 20 pence worth of gobstoppers. The assistant pulled out a step-ladder, climbed up to the top shelf, carefully took down the jar, counted out the gobstoppers, re-stoppered the jar, climbed back up the ladder and replaced the sweets on the top shelf. After taking the lad's money, she asked the second boy what he would like. 'Twenty pence worth of gobstoppers, please,' he replied. So she got out the ladder again, got down the jar and counted out the sweets. Before she put the jar back, she turned to the third boy and said, 'I suppose you'd like 20 pence worth of gobstoppers too, would you?'

The boy shook his head, so the assistant went back up the ladder to replace the jar. 'Right,' she said, when she'd got down again, 'what can I get you, then?'

'I'd like 50 pence worth of gobstoppers, please,' replied the boy.

ANGRY MOTHER: I sent my son out to buy a kilo of strawberries but when he got home and I weighed them he'd only got half a kilo. Is there something wrong with your scales?

GREENGROCER: There's nothing wrong with my scales, madam. Have you tried weighing your son?

SIGN OUTSIDE ANOTHER GREENGROCER'S: Our scales are accurate – no two weighs about it.

SIGN OUTSIDE A HEALTH FOOD SHOP: Closed on account of sickness.

SHOPPER: I'd like some two-handed cheese, please.
SHOPKEEPER: What do you mean, 'two-handed cheese'?
SHOPPER: You know, the sort you eat with one hand while holding your nose with the other.

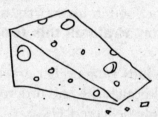

Where does Superman shop for food?
In the supermarket.

Where does Dr Who shop for food?
In a dalek-atessen.

What romantic and tuneful thing do you need in a supermarket?
A Chopin Liszt.

DANNY: Did you hear what happened in the supermarket last week?
ANNIE: No, what?
DANNY: A customer was strangled by five fish fingers.

DELICATESSEN OWNER: I've got frogs' legs, spiced liver, cold tongue . . .
SHOPPER: I don't want to hear about your problems, I just want to buy some ham.

What did the fat man say as he paid for all the food in his supermarket trolley?
'I'm afraid all this food will go to waist.'

A lady rang up her greengrocer to say that although she had ordered 12 peaches, he had only delivered 11.

'I know, madam,' he replied, 'but one was bad so I threw it away.'

How can you stop the food you buy in your week's shopping from going bad?
Eat it!

What's Cooking?

BRIAN: Is your mum a good cook?
RYAN: Not really. Last night she burnt the salad.

How can you stop rice from sticking when you cook it?
Boil each grain separately.

How do you make an apple puff?
Chase it round the garden.

Did you hear about the young cook who thought that cold boiled ham was boiled ham with cold water poured over it?

MOTHER: Yesterday there were ten strawberry tarts in the larder, and today there's only one. Why?
SON: I don't know. I suppose it must have been at the back where I didn't see it.

Did you hear about the silly cook who boiled an egg for 20 minutes and complained that it still wasn't soft?

SON: Do you like baked apples?
MOTHER: Yes. Why?
SON: The orchard's on fire.

How do you make a jam turnover?
Push it off the table.

TIM: We had roast boar for dinner at Grandad's.
JIM: Wild?
TIM: Well, it wasn't too pleased.

MOTHER: I thought I asked you to watch the rice and see when it boiled over?
DILLY: I did! It boiled over at half past seven.

FIRST COOK: Say something sweet to me.
SECOND COOK: Lemon meringue pie.

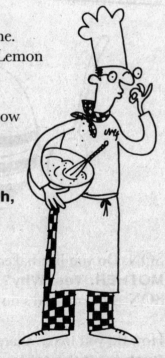

FRENCH CHEF: How do our French dishes compare with your English ones?
ENGLISH CHEF: Oh, they break just as easily.

What does a chef do if someone faints in their kitchen?
Gives them the quiche of life.

Mrs Jolly had cooked a chicken for dinner and little Jilly Jolly asked, 'Please may I have the wishbone?'

'Not until you've eaten up all your vegetables,' replied her mother.

'But, Mum,' answered Jilly, 'I want to wish I don't have to eat them all.'

What do you get if you cross a plate of stew with a cowboy?
Hopalong casserole.

FATHER: What kind of meat is this?
MOTHER: It's venison.
FATHER: Is it expensive?
MOTHER: Yes, it's deer.

Why is roast pork like an old radio?
They both have a lot of crackling.

MR WHITTLE: Are you sure this ham is cured?
MRS WHITTLE: Oh yes. Why?
MR WHITTLE: It still looks rather ill to me.

Why did the pizza climb on to the roof?
It'd heard the meal was on the house.

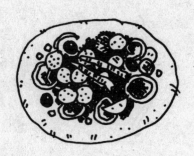

How do monkeys make toast?
They put it under the gorilla.

What's as tall as a tower block and contains thousands of eggs?
A multi-storey omelette.

What would you get if you crossed a chicken with an electric organ?
Hammond eggs.

How can you spell ham and eggs in three letters?
MNX.

MRS MYRTLE: Cuthbert! Wake up! There's a burglar downstairs and he's eating that steak and kidney pie I made for tomorrow's lunch.
MR MYRTLE: What shall I do first – call the police or phone for an ambulance?

Why did the family eat all the white meat off the chicken?
To make a clean breast of it.

JENNY: I'm not to go to cookery lessons any more.
MUM: Oh, why not?
JENNY: Because I burnt something.
MUM: That doesn't sound too serious. What did you burn?
JENNY: I burnt the cookery classroom down.

GRANDMA: You've left all your crusts, Sammy. When I was your age I ate every one of mine.
SAMMY: Do you still like crusts, Granny?
GRANDMA: Yes.
SAMMY: Well, you can have mine.

A tramp knocked on a door and asked the woman who opened it if she could spare any food. 'Didn't I give you a meat pie last week?' she asked.

'Yes,' replied the tramp, 'but I'm better now.'

BROTHER, TASTING: *What* kind of fruit pie was it you made?
SISTER: Well, I made two. What does it taste of?
BROTHER: Old tea leaves.
SISTER: Then that's the plum pie. The apple pie tastes of soap.

What flour do pixies use?
Elf-raising flour.

Mother caught little Herbert in the larder.
'And what do you think you're up to?' she
asked.
   'I'm up to my sixth scone,' he replied.

What's short, green, and goes camping?
A boy sprout.

Where did the baby cabbage come from?
The stalk brought it.

Where do you find chilli peppers?
At the North Pole.

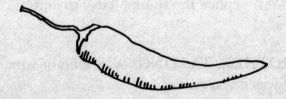

What do you call two rows of cabbages?
A dual cabbageway.

How can you calculate the colour of a cabbage?
With a green gauge.

HIL: I made a lovely chicken pie and the dog's eaten it.
PHIL: Never mind, Mum'll buy us another dog.

MOTHER: No, Freddie, you can't have any more supper. It's bad to go to sleep on a full stomach.
FREDDIE: But I can lie on my side, can't I?

MOTHER: This lettuce tastes a bit funny, are you sure you washed it as I asked you?
JIMMY: Yes, look, you can still see the soap!

Where were chips first fried?
In Greece.

VEGETARIAN: I've lived on nothing but vegetables for years.
HIS FRIEND: I've lived on Earth all my life.

What do you get if you cross sugar and egg-whites with a monkey?
Meringue-utan.

How do you make gold soup?
Well, you start with 14 carats.

What did the egg say to the food mixer?
'I know when I'm beaten.'

Custard Pies

What can a whole custard pie do that half a custard pie can't do?
Look round.

WAYNE: You remind me of a pie.
JAYNE: Because I'm all sweetness and light?
WAYNE: No, because you've got some crust.

Why are grapes never lonely?
Because they hang around in bunches.

What do you get if you cross apples with an aeroplane?
Pie in the sky.

What did the man say who had jelly in one ear and custard in the other?

'You'll have to speak up, I'm a trifle deaf.'

What do you get if you cross a strawberry with an elk?

Strawberry mousse.

What's yellow, fuzzy and travels at 200 mph?

A fuel-injected peach.

JEFF: Why do you call your girlfriend Peach? Is it because she's so pretty?

JOHN: No, because she's got a heart of stone.

Why did the banana go out with the prune?

Because he couldn't find a date.

What should you do with a blue banana?
Try to cheer it up.

Why don't bananas snore?
They don't want to wake up the rest of the bunch.

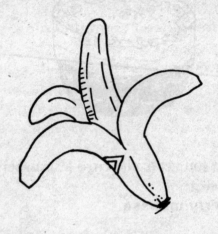

Why did the silly man lose his job in the fruit-packing factory?
He kept throwing away the bent bananas.

How do you make a banana split?
Cut it in two.

Which side of a gooseberry is the hairiest?
The outside.

How do you make an apple crumble?
Put it through a potato masher.

What's round, orange, and can't sit down?
A seatless satsuma.

How can you tell the time by a fruit?
Eat an orange and count the pips.

An accident happened to my brother Jim
When somebody threw a tomato at him.
Tomatoes are squashy and don't hurt the skin –
But this one was specially packed in a tin.

What nut has no shell?
A doughnut.

What did one tomato say to the other
tomato?
**'If you'd kept your mouth shut we
wouldn't be in this pickle.'**

What happens to tomatoes in the autumn?
People eat what they can, and can what they can't.

Why did the gardener plant knives alongside his potatoes?
He was trying to grow chips.

MOTHER: Why is your little sister so unhappy?
JIMMY: Because I wouldn't give her my sandwich.
MOTHER: Is hers finished?
JIMMY: Yes, and she was upset when I ate that, too.

Why did the girl sleep with a packet of sugar under her pillow?
So she could have sweet dreams.

NEIGHBOUR: Why are you planting onions with your potatoes?
GARDENER: The onions will make the potatoes' eyes water and I shan't have to water them.

NEIGHBOUR: Do you have a potato patch?
GARDENER: Why, do you have a leaking potato?

CUSTOMER: Those potatoes you sold me yesterday are full of eyes.
SHOPKEEPER: Well, you did say you wanted enough to see you through the week.

What did the potato say when it was wrapped up and put in the oven?
'Foiled again!'

What happened to the woman who ate a lot of sugar?
She got a lump in the throat.

MOTHER: Why did you mop up your tea with your cake?
ANDY: Well, you did say it was sponge cake.

73

What do police patrols like in their cakes?
Traffic jam.

FAN: What are your favourite roles?
ACTOR: Hamlet, King Lear, tuna and cucumber.

What's yellow and leaps from cake to cake?
Tarzipan.

BOY ON HOLIDAY: Do these cows really give milk?
FARMER: Well, you do have to squeeze it out of them.

What looks like half a cake?
The other half.

Which king of England burnt the cakes?
Alfred the Grate.

Why did the lady have her hair in a bun?
Because she had her nose in a hamburger.

What did the biscuit say when his friend ran across the road?
'Crumbs!'

A lady found a small boy sobbing in the street and asked him why he was crying.

'I was thirsty,' he wept, 'so I swapped my dog for a can of lemonade.'

'And now you wish you had him back, I suppose?' asked the lady.

'Yes,' sniffed the boy.

'Because you love him?' asked the lady.

'No,' howled the boy. 'Because I'm thirsty again!'

What is lemonade?
It's when you help an elderly lemon across the road.

EX-SAILOR: Once when I was shipwrecked I had to live on a tin of sardines for a week.
BORED LISTENER: It's a wonder you didn't fall off.

How do you make a lemon drop?
Shake the tree hard.

What's a monster's favourite drink?
Demon-ade.

What turns without moving?
Milk, when it turns sour.

CUSTOMER: Yesterday's milk was very watery.

MILKMAN: The cow must have been out in the rain.

When is it OK to drink milk from a saucer?
When you're a cat.

What has only one horn and gives a lot of milk?
A milk lorry.

Did you hear about the schoolboy who was asked to write an essay about milk and only wrote two lines? His excuse was that he was writing about condensed milk.

FATHER: I've just found two 10p pieces, three pennies and a 20p piece in my gravy!
MOTHER: Well, you did say you wanted some change in your meals.

What do ghosts eat for dinner?
Spookhetti.

Why did the man order alphabet soup?
He liked to read while he was eating.

How can a cook make her cakes light?
Soak them in petrol.

What's thick, yellow, and very dangerous?
Shark-infested custard.

What did one sardine say to the other?
'Can you move over a bit, you're squashing me.'

Pot Luck

FIRST CANNIBAL: Do you like beans?
SECOND CANNIBAL: Yes.
FIRST CANNIBAL: What kind?
SECOND CANNIBAL: Human bein's.

Two men were unwrapping their sandwiches. 'Oh, no,' said the first, 'not cheese and pickle again.'

'Don't you like cheese and pickle?' asked the second.

'I hate them!' said the first.

'So why don't you ask your wife to make you something else?'

'Oh my wife doesn't make my sandwiches,' replied the first. 'I do!'

FIRST CANNIBAL: I just don't know what to make of my husband nowadays.
SECOND CANNIBAL: How about a hotpot?

What's yellow and white and goes at 120 mph?
A train driver's egg sandwich.

Why can't you put an elephant in a sandwich?
It's too heavy to lift.

What's the difference between a country bumpkin and a Welsh rarebit?
One's easy to cheat, the other's cheesy to eat.

How can you tell if there's an elephant in your custard?
It's even more lumpy than usual.

What did the mayonnaise say to the fridge?
'Close the door, I'm dressing.'

What was purple and wanted to rule the world?
Alexander the Grape.

TEACHER: Can you name six things with milk in them?
ANNIE: Er, cheese, yogurt, and four cows.

BEN: Did I tell you the joke about the butter?
KEN: No, what is it?
BEN: I'd better not say. You might spread it around.

What cake wanted to rule the world?
Attila the Bun.

What do jelly babies wear on their feet?
Gum boots.

How can you avoid starvation on a desert island?
By eating the sand which is (sandwiches) there.

CUSTOMER: Butcher, have you got a sheep's head?
BUTCHER: No, madam, it's just the way I part my hair.

How do you make a chicken stew?
Keep it waiting for an hour or two.

MOTHER: How many times must I tell you to come out of that larder!
JOHNNY: No more, Mum, it's empty!

MOTHER: Have you filled the salt cellar yet?
MARY: No, Mum, I couldn't get all the salt through the little hole in the top.

His mum gave Larry two apples, a big one and a small one, and said, 'Now, Larry, share these with your sister.'

So Larry gave the small apple to his sister and took a bite out of the large one himself.

'Hmm,' said his sister. 'You're not very polite. If Mum had given me the apples I'd have given you the big one and kept the small one for myself.'

'But that's what you've got,' replied Larry. 'So what are you whingeing about?'

What do you get if you cross gunpowder with an egg?
A boom-meringue.

I eat my peas with honey,
I've done it all my life.
It makes the peas taste funny
But it keeps them on the knife.

KAREN: Just think, a box of chocolates, an ice cream sundae and a delicious cream cake for 50p.
SHARON: Did you get all that for 50p?
KAREN: No, but just think . . .

What kinds of fish do you need to make a shoe?
A sole and an eel.

How many apples can you put in an empty bag?
Only one – after that the bag isn't empty any more.

What happened when the red sauce chased the brown sauce?
It couldn't ketchup.

What's green and white and bounces?
A spring onion.

What do you get if you cross
rabbits with leeks?
Bunions.

What's the quickest way to
gain weight?
**Eat a plum and you'll
gain a stone.**

MRS ROUND: I'm on a
seafood diet.
MRS THIN: Really?
MRS ROUND: Yes,
the more I see food the more I eat it.

A fishmonger was chalking a sign for his shop
that read: 'Fresh Fish Sold Here Today'. A
passerby stopped and said, 'You don't need to
put "today" on your sign, do you? I mean,
you're not selling it yesterday or tomorrow,
are you?'

'No,' replied the fishmonger. 'I suppose
you're right.' And he rubbed out the word
'today'.

'And you don't need "here" either, do

you?' persisted the passerby. 'I mean, you're not selling it anywhere else, are you?'

'I suppose not,' answered the fishmonger. And he rubbed out the word 'here'.

'And for that matter you don't need "sold", do you? You're not likely to be giving it away.'

'Certainly not,' agreed the fishmonger, rubbing out the word 'sold'.

'And I wouldn't put "fresh", either. You wouldn't be selling it if it weren't fresh, would you?'

'That's true,' agreed the fishmonger, getting his duster ready.

'Just one more thing,' said the passerby. 'I wouldn't bother to put "fish", either, if I were you – I could smell it right down the road!'

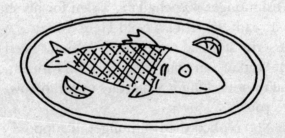

MILLY: Would you like to try a boiled duck egg?
TILLY: Only if you quack it for me.

Young Freddie was having tea with his granny. 'Would you like some bread and butter?' she asked.

'Yes, please,' answered Freddie. And when she passed him the plate of bread and butter, he said, 'Thank you.'

'You are a polite little boy,' said Granny, pleased. 'I like to hear you say "please" and "thank you".'

'Good,' said Freddie. 'And if you'd like to hear me say them again, you could offer me some jam to go with it.'

Terri was going to see her friend Jerry who was in hospital. 'I've brought you some of your favourite chocolates,' she said.

'Oh, thanks,' said Jerry, opening the box. His face dropped. 'But it's half empty,' he said.

'Ah,' said Terri, 'well, you see, they're my favourite chocolates too.'

MOTHER: How many times have I told you not to reach across the table for the salt and pepper? Haven't you got a tongue in your head?
MOIRA: Yes, but my arm's longer.

What's a frog's favourite sweet?
A lollihop.

Did Adam and Eve have a date?
No, they had an apple.

What's furry and tastes of peppermint?
A Polo bear.

What do frogs like to drink?
Croaka Cola.

What do computer programmers eat for supper?
Microchips.

COOKERY TEACHER: Now be careful, Louise, remember most accidents at home happen in the kitchen.
LOUISE, SIGHING: I know. I have to eat them.

What's green, prickly, and goes putt, putt, putt?
An outboard gooseberry.

What's an apricot?
What a baby monkey sleeps in.

The teacher was trying to make maths more interesting. So she said to the class, 'If I slice up two bananas and two apples into ten pieces each, what will I have?'

Smarty-pants Susie put her hand up. 'Please, Miss,' she said, 'a fruit salad.'

DEREK: Why are you eating a banana with the skin on?
ERIC: Because I know what's inside.

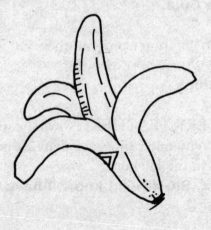

What did the boy banana say to the girl banana?
You appeal to me.

What sits in a fruit bowl and shouts for help?
A damson in distress.

What's green and goes boing, boing, boing?
Spring cabbage.

Why did the orange go to the doctor?
Because it wasn't peeling well.

What do you get if you cross a bee with
minced meat?
A humburger.

If cheese comes on top of a hamburger, what
comes after cheese?
Mice.

What's green and makes cheeky remarks?
A fresh vegetable.

What's yellow and writes letters?
A ballpoint banana.

BILL: Where did you get the recipe for this cake?
JILL: I cut it out of a magazine.
BILL: Are you sure you used the right side of the page? The other side tells you how to make a rock garden.

What do you call a very large pumpkin?
A plumpkin.

What's made of chocolate and found on the seabed?
An oyster egg.

What fruit plays snooker?
A cue-cumber.

What are round, green and smell of fish?
Brussels sprats.

Why does crossing a yellow fruit with a green
vegetable make you sad?
Because it makes you melon-cauli.

And, finally, what happens to people who eat
too many sweets?
They take up two seats!

A selected list of titles available from Macmillan and Pan Books

The prices shown below are correct at the time of going to press. However, Macmillan Publishers reserve the right to show new retail prices on covers which may differ from those previously advertised.

The Knock Knock Joke Book Sandy Ransford	0 330 37514 8	£2.99
Spooky Jokes Sandy Ransford	0 330 39061 9	£2.99
2001: A Joke Odyssey **The Millennium Joke Book** Sandy Ransford	0 330 34988 0	£3.99
School Jokes Sandy Ransford	0 330 39222 0	£2.99
Absolutely Mental 1 Rowland Morgan	0 330 48172 X	£2.99
Absolutely Mental 2 Rowland Morgan	0 330 48173 8	£2.99

All Macmillan titles can be ordered at your local bookshop or are available by post from:

Book Service by Post
PO Box 29, Douglas, Isle of Man IM99 1BQ

Credit cards accepted. For details:
Telephone: 01624 675137
Fax: 01624 670923
E-mail: bookshop@enterprise.net

Free postage and packing in the UK.
Overseas customers: add £1 per book (paperback)